GW01424384

Original title:
City of Dreams

Copyright © 2024 Creative Arts Management OÜ
All rights reserved.

Author: Tim Wood

ISBN HARDBACK: 978-9916-88-134-7
ISBN PAPERBACK: 978-9916-88-135-4

Concrete Gardens of Longing

In the city's heart, dreams take root,
Concrete blooms, seeking the sun's pursuit.
Whispers of hope in the cracks of the gray,
Gardens of longing, where shadows play.

Beneath the steel and the weight of despair,
Tendrils of green reach for warmth in the air.
Each petal a story, each leaf a song,
In this urban expanse, we still belong.

Rhythms of Urban Resilience

Trains rumble past, a heartbeat so strong,
Traffic's a symphony, bustling along.
Voices interweave, a vibrant refrain,
Dancing through struggles, embracing the strain.

Neon lights flicker, igniting the night,
In every challenge, we find our delight.
Resilience is woven in every street,
A melody crafted by all that we meet.

Metropolises of the Mind

Thoughts like skyscrapers, reaching so high,
Visions unfolding, like clouds in the sky.
Each avenue leads to a place unexplored,
Metropolises growing, with dreams as our sword.

Bridges of ideas span over the void,
Casting reflections where fears are destroyed.
In the landscape of thought, we roam free and wild,
Finding the silence where chaos has smiled.

Reflections in Glass and Grit

Mirrored surfaces capture our past,
Windows to worlds, both fragile and vast.
Grit in the alleyways tells tales untold,
Stories of lives that the city enfold.

In each shard of glass, a life can be seen,
Fragments of being, where struggles convene.
Reflections of hope, through layers of time,
In the city's embrace, we find our climb.

Parables of a Paved Paradise

Concrete dreams under neon skies,
Silent whispers where nature lies.
Footsteps echo on the busy street,
Lost in a rhythm, a heart's quiet beat.

Skyscrapers rise, blocking the sun,
Chasing shadows, we always run.
Hopes paved over like ancient trails,
In search of freedom, the spirit fails.

Nature's song drowned by engines' roar,
Promises of peace we can't ignore.
In this paradise made of stone,
We find ourselves, yet feel alone.

Yet in the cracks, wildflowers bloom,
Defying chaos, dispelling gloom.
A parable of life, so bittersweet,
In a paved paradise, we seek our seat.

Stars Over Simulated Cities

Artificial lights paint the night,
Real stars hidden, out of sight.
Screens flicker with dreams so bright,
In simulated worlds, we take flight.

Cars glide smoothly, no lull or stop,
Yet inside, hearts feel the drop.
Chasing pixels, we build our fate,
But a longing for more we can't negate.

Beneath the surface, life pulses strong,
Echoes of nature sing a song.
The urban jungle, both grand and small,
In this kingdom we read a tale of all.

Beyond the buildings that pierce the sky,
The stars ignite, for those who try.
In every corner, a truth exists,
In simulated cities, our dreams persist.

Beneath Layers of Humanity

Faces passing in a crowded place,
Stories hidden in every trace.
Search for kindness in hurried glances,
Beneath the layers, life advances.

Worn-out shoes on uneven ground,
Silent struggles often go unbound.
In crowded rooms, we feel apart,
Yet every echo holds a heart.

Voices lost in the city's hum,
Every heartbeat a distant drum.
Connection sought in fleeting moments,
Layers peel back, hidden components.

Beneath the noise, a whisper calls,
In shared silence, our spirit stalls.
For in the depth of humanity's core,
Resides a truth, we all adore.

Tapestries of Light and Shadow

Colors dance on a canvas bright,
Woven stories of day and night.
Shadows linger in corners deep,
Tales of life, both awake and asleep.

Flickering flames cast gentle hues,
Life's rich palette, the dreams we choose.
Threads of laughter, strands of sorrow,
In every weave, a brand new tomorrow.

Time unravels as moments blend,
In this tapestry, we find a friend.
Bright threads pull us toward the light,
While shadows remind us of the night.

Each layer tells of struggles faced,
In every stitch, a memory placed.
Together we create this art,
A tapestry of light, a shared heart.

Above the Roofs

Skyscrapers touch the endless blue,
Dreams and hopes soar, old and new.
Whispers of time echo in the air,
Life's tapestry woven without a care.

Birds dance lightly, shadows shift,
Moments stolen, nature's gift.
Clouds drift by, a fleeting play,
Above the roofs, we find our way.

Beneath the Stars

In the night, a blanket spread,
Twinkling lights overhead.
Dreamers gather, stories unfold,
Mysteries of the cosmos told.

Hearts beat softly, breaths align,
Underneath the vast divine.
Hope ignites like distant flames,
Beneath the stars, no one's the same.

Chronicles of the Pavement

Footsteps echo on the street,
Every path a tale discreet.
Concrete whispers, history calls,
In the shadows, the city sprawls.

Colors blend where lives converge,
In every corner, souls emerge.
Silent stories, laughter hides,
Chronicles of life, timeless tides.

Windows to Infinite Possibilities

Glass panes spark with bright allure,
Reflections dance, futures pure.
Every window tells a tale,
Of dreams that dare, of hopes that sail.

Frames of life, vast and wide,
Open hearts, paths to guide.
In every glance, a chance bestowed,
Windows open, adventures road.

Threads of Life in the Urban Fabric

Woven tightly, lives entwine,
Colors vibrant, stories shine.
Every thread holds a key,
To the fabric of you and me.

Moments stitched with love and fear,
Comfort found, together near.
In the bustle, we unite,
Threads of life, a tapestry bright.

The Mirage of Tomorrow

In the haze where dreams reside,
Visions dance like waves on tide.
Echoes whisper of what's to come,
Yet time drifts on, a silent drum.

Through the mist, we chase the light,
Fingers grasping, hearts in flight.
But shadows loom, our doubts unfurl,
In the mirage, we spin and twirl.

Stories Written in Graffiti

On city walls, tales collide,
Colors bleed where truth can't hide.
Each stroke breathes life, a voice so bold,
An urban canvas, stories told.

From broken hearts to dreams anew,
In every splash, the world's view.
Silent cries and joyful screams,
Graffiti speaks of shattered dreams.

Hopes Raised on Steel Beams

High above, where eagles soar,
Steel beams bridge what lies in store.
Dreams constructed, futures gleam,
On sturdy bones, we build our dream.

With courage, we reach for the sky,
Against the odds, we learn to fly.
In the heights, our spirits beam,
Each footstep solid, grounded team.

Beyond the Flickering Bulbs

In the dim light, secrets glow,
Flickering bulbs where whispers flow.
Hiding tales of love and loss,
In shadows deep, we bear the cross.

Each moment caught in fading light,
Fragments held in the night's quiet flight.
Beyond the glow, the stories hide,
In the flicker, our fears abide.

Urban Reveries

In the city's pulse, dreams collide,
Neon lights dance, secrets confide.
Footsteps echo on the crowded streets,
Every heart races, each moment beats.

Cafes hum with laughter and sighs,
Beneath the sprawling, open skies.
Stories woven in the night's embrace,
Urban reveries, time can't erase.

Windows flicker, narratives flow,
Life's vibrant canvas, an endless show.
Voices blend in a sweet refrain,
In this urban realm, joy and pain.

Beneath the concrete, hope is sown,
In every heart, a seed is grown.
Together we walk, through night and day,
In urban reveries, we find our way.

Metropolis of Whispers

Silent stories in shadows creep,
Echoes of secrets that the night keeps.
Footfalls soft on alleys worn,
In a metropolis where dreams are born.

Street lamps flicker, casting pools of light,
Guiding wanderers through the night.
Whispers gather in the cool, crisp air,
Tales of longing in the silence laid bare.

Between the buildings, a heartbeat hums,
In every corner, another voice comes.
Café conversations, laughter shared,
In this metropolis, souls are bared.

Time unfolds with each whispered thought,
In hidden spaces, connections are sought.
A city alive, in night's gentle bliss,
Metropolis of whispers, where moments kiss.

Shadows on Concrete

Sunset paints the skyline gray,
Longing shadows begin to play.
Concrete giants tower high,
Beneath their gaze, the lost sigh.

Flickering signs in twilight glow,
Silhouettes move, fast or slow.
In the alleys, stories weave,
Shadows linger, memories grieve.

Pavements whisper of lives once lived,
In the darkness, hope survives.
With each heartbeat, the city sighs,
Shadows dance beneath the skies.

In the night, new dreams are born,
From the ashes, souls adorn.
Together we tread, through the unknown,
In shadows on concrete, we find home.

Skylines of Hope

A rising dawn, the skyline glows,
In every window, a dream bestows.
Light breaks through the quiet night,
Painting the world in hues of bright.

Each tower stands, a testament strong,
To resilience found in the city's song.
Through struggles faced, we lift our gaze,
In skylines of hope, our spirits blaze.

The horizon calls with promises new,
In every block, opportunities grew.
Together we climb, hands intertwined,
In the urban sprawl, our futures aligned.

Skyward we reach, unyielding and bold,
In this landscape of stories untold.
With every heartbeat, our spirits cope,
In the skyline's embrace, we find hope.

The Odyssey of Aspiration

In the distance, dreams arise,
Chasing whispers in the skies.
With every step, the heart takes flight,
Guided by stars in the quiet night.

Paths are winding, shadows play,
Hurdles faced along the way.
Yet hope ignites the weary soul,
Onward still, the ultimate goal.

A journey paved with doubts and fears,
Yet each obstacle simply clears.
With persistence, the summit gleams,
For in the heart live all our dreams.

So rise, awaken, and dare to roam,
The world awaits; your dreams are home.
In every step, a story unfolds,
The odyssey of aspiration, bold.

Essence of Concrete Dreams

In the city's heart, a pulse so deep,
Concrete visions awaken from sleep.
Steel and glass become the frame,
Where every spark ignites the flame.

Silent whispers in urban sprawl,
Echoes of hope in the rise and fall.
Every corner, a story to tell,
Of dreams that grew, of wishes that swell.

Underneath the shadows cast high,
Yearning for more, while reaching sky.
Foundations strong, yet delicate,
In the fabric, dreams we create.

An essence captured in each design,
In the heartbeat of the urban line.
Concrete dreams that rise and gleam,
A testament to life's vivid theme.

Portraits of the Skyline

Against the dusk, the towers stand,
Brushstrokes bold by human hand.
Each silhouette a tale untold,
In the canvas of the night, behold.

Colors dance as light takes flight,
Whispers of day blend into night.
Windows glimmer, stories shared,
Each reflection a moment declared.

In every building, dreams reside,
With every curve, a heart's confide.
Portraits crafted in shadows' play,
The skyline breathes, come what may.

Look up high, let spirit soar,
In the skyline, find so much more.
A gallery framed by hopes and dreams,
The city lives in vibrant seams.

Transformations Under the Urban Gaze

Beneath the arches, shadows shift,
Life transforms in every gift.
The city's rhythm, a constant flow,
In every alley, stories grow.

Past meets present, a dance unfolds,
Old bricks whispering tales of gold.
In the labyrinth, we find our grace,
Identities blend in this shared space.

Moments captured, lives entwined,
With every heartbeat, hope defined.
Ultimately shaped by dreams we chase,
Under the urban gaze, we embrace.

Together we rise, the future in hand,
In transformations bold, we boldly stand.
A tapestry woven through time and space,
In unity's vision, we find our place.

Nightfall in Concrete Jungles

The city breathes as shadows creep,
Neon dreams in silence sleep.
A symphony of distant sounds,
Lost in echoes, heart abounds.

Streetlights flicker, guiding home,
Amid the steel, the spirits roam.
Darkened paths, secrets unfold,
Whispers of stories, yet untold.

Rain-soaked pavements glisten bright,
Reflections dance in flecks of light.
A canvas painted, rich and deep,
In night's embrace, the world we keep.

Stars concealed in urban skies,
Still, the heart of city sighs.
In every corner, life ignites,
Nightfall brings new dreams in sights.

Wanderlust in the Urban Maze

Amid the skyscrapers, dreams take flight,
Endless paths beneath the light.
Every corner, stories wait,
Each step forward, weave your fate.

Subway hums a lullaby,
As weary souls drift and sigh.
Through crowded streets, adventure calls,
Wanderlust ignites, the spirit sprawls.

Art on walls in vibrant hues,
Every mural tells the news.
A city's heartbeat, loud and clear,
In urban jungles, lose your fear.

From dawn to dusk, the thrill expands,
Hands outstretched, take a chance.
Embrace the chaos, let it flow,
In the maze of life, seeds we sow.

A Symphony of Sirens

Night awakens with a call,
City's heartbeat, rises and falls.
Sirens wail, a haunting tune,
Echoes linger beneath the moon.

Voices merge in vibrant streets,
Rhythms pulse, the city beats.
Every note tells tales of strife,
A symphony of urban life.

In the chaos, beauty lies,
Harmony in lullabies.
Moments fleeting, swift as light,
Captured in the city's night.

Underneath the star-clad sky,
Melodies of dreams still fly.
With every note, hearts combine,
In this symphony, souls entwine.

Mosaics of Light and Starlight

Windows shine like scattered stars,
Reflecting dreams from near to far.
Colorful mosaics fill the night,
Fragments of joy, pieces of light.

Pavements spark with every step,
Memories whispered, secrets kept.
During twilight, shadows dance,
Intertwining fate and chance.

The urban pulse, a guiding force,
In every street, life finds its course.
Art and motion blend and sway,
In vibrant hues, the night holds play.

As starlight falls on busy streets,
In every heart, the city beats.
A patchwork quilt of dreams and sights,
Mosaics of life in sparkling lights.

Ballet of the Twilight

In the hush where shadows play,
Dancers twirl at close of day.
Silken gowns catch the dim light,
Stars awaken, fade from sight.

Whispers glide on evening air,
The world forgetting all its care.
Moonlight bathes the stage in glow,
As time dances soft and slow.

Spin and leap, a fleeting dream,
Echoing the night's sweet theme.
In this quiet, magic sways,
A ballet born of twilight's gaze.

As the darkness holds it tight,
Every heart finds peace tonight.
Underneath the sky's embrace,
Life unfolds with gentle grace.

Portraits of the Unseen

In the corners, stories lie,
Faded frames that whisper why.
Faces lost in time's cruel grasp,
Holding on to moments past.

Veiled truths in every glance,
Ghosts of history's last dance.
Colors blur, the edges fray,
As shadows blend with light of day.

Each portrait tells a tale untold,
Of joys deep and sorrows bold.
In silence, they keep their grace,
Inviting us to seek their trace.

Layers thick with joy and pain,
Framed with sunlight, framed with rain.
The unseen speaks through time's lens,
Binding us as it transcends.

Future Found in the Ruins

Among the stones, a seed must grow,
In echoes of what once we know.
Crumbled walls, a whispered prayer,
Hope rises with the earth laid bare.

Nature paints with gentle hand,
Life reclaiming what was planned.
In every crack, a story waits,
New beginnings open gates.

Old bones shelter dreams anew,
In the dust, a radiant view.
Fortunes lost, yet not forgot,
From the ashes, peace is sought.

The past, a canvas worn and frayed,
Embracing life where once it played.
For in the ruins, seeds take flight,
Future born from endless night.

Whispers between the Walls

Secrets cradle in the beams,
Silent echoes of lost dreams.
Each heartbeat stirs the quiet air,
A tale woven with tender care.

Flickering lights cast shadows long,
Holding whispers of a song.
Voices linger, soft and near,
Hushed replies that only we hear.

Memories in every crease,
Longing shades that never cease.
In this space, the past resides,
Wrapped in whispers where love hides.

Through the cracks, the stories flow,
Threads of time that gently sew.
Between the walls, life's refrain,
Whispers softly call again.

The Pulse of Ambition

In the quiet nights, dreams ignite,
Whispers of hope, reaching for height.
Every heartbeat echoes, chasing a flame,
With every step forward, a brand-new name.

Through valleys of doubt, the spirit will soar,
Climbing each mountain, yearning for more.
In the shadows of fear, courage will stand,
Together we forge, an unyielding band.

The vision is clear, a future so bright,
With passion as fuel, we conquer the night.
In the pulse of ambition, life finds its song,
Together we journey, where we all belong.

With stars as our guide, we write our own fate,
In the dance of the brave, we celebrate.
Through trials and triumphs, we carve our way,
The pulse of ambition propels us each day.

Stardust on Pavement

On cobbled streets where dreams collide,
Sparkling fragments of hopes reside.
Under city lights, a tale unfolds,
Stardust whispers of treasures untold.

With every footstep, we leave a trace,
A dance with shadows, a fleeting grace.
The rhythm of life in the nighttime air,
Woven together, there's magic to share.

Beneath the arches of time's embrace,
We gather memories, a sacred place.
With laughter and tears, we paint the night,
Stardust on pavement, a shimmering sight.

Through alleyways narrow and corners bright,
The stories of souls converge in the light.
In every heartbeat, a promise remains,
Stardust on pavement, where love never wanes.

Skylights and Shadows

In the morning glow, shadows retreat,
Skylights awake, illuminating the street.
The world comes alive, a canvas anew,
Painting the moments in every hue.

With laughter like music, we stroll hand in hand,
Creating our symphony, a life so grand.
In the gaps of the day, dreams softly blend,
Skylights above, where hopes never end.

As twilight descends, shadows expand,
They cradle the night like a gentle hand.
In the heart of the city, where secrets reside,
Skylights and shadows, forever our guide.

Each flicker of light, a story to tell,
In the dance of the day, we weave our spell.
Through the ebb and the flow, we journey on through,
Skylights and shadows, forever in view.

The Symphony of Sidewalks

Along the cracked sidewalks, footsteps resound,
A symphony brews in the heart of the town.
Every sound tells a story, a life lived in tune,
Under the gaze of the silver-lined moon.

From whispers of lovers to children at play,
Harmony rises in the light of the day.
The rhythm of life, both tender and bold,
In the dance of the crowds, a dream to behold.

With melodies drifting through the evening air,
Each moment a note in a world that we share.
As twilight embraces, the music transforms,
The symphony swells, with the evening's soft charms.

Every cautioning crack, every rustle of leaves,
Sings of the stories the side-walk believes.
Together we march, where our hearts intertwine,
In the symphony of sidewalks, forever we shine.

Beneath the Roofs of Reality

Concrete towers loom above,
Their shadows drape the streets.
Life whispers in the corners,
Trapped dreams caught in beats.

Windows flicker like fireflies,
Silent tales they hold within.
Each laugh and tear a chapter,
Beneath this skin of sin.

The pulse of countless stories,
Weaving paths of hopes and fears.
In the heart of stone and steel,
We've built our lives and tears.

Amidst the rush and noise,
We seek the quiet grace.
Beneath the roofs of reality,
We find our sacred space.

Dreams Woven in High-Rises

Skyward aspirations rise,
In steel, glass, and light.
Each floor holds hidden visions,
Chasing dreams by night.

Laughter flows through hallways,
Echoing in the air.
Whispers of forgotten hopes,
Dance beyond despair.

In every window glimmers,
A glimpse of what could be.
A world of endless journeys,
Inspire the heart to see.

High above the bustling chaos,
We carve our own path true.
Dreams woven in high-rises,
As stars weave skies anew.

Murmurs of the Urban Wilderness

Pavement cracks like ancient roots,
Life emerges to defy.
In the brush of wildflowers,
A vibrant rebel cry.

Steel and stone surround us,
Yet nature finds a way.
Among the shouts and chaos,
Sweet birdsong greets the day.

Graffiti blooms on concrete,
Colors clash, yet they blend.
In the heart of the city,
Murmurs start and seldom end.

Listen close to the whispers,
Of the life that dares to thrive.
Murmurs of the urban wild,
Reminding us we're alive.

Beyond the Horizon of Noise

In the hush of dying twilight,
When the world exhales slow.
Beyond the horizon of noise,
Peace begins to grow.

Flickering lights fade to shadows,
A gentle sigh of night.
Beneath the vast expanse,
Stars awaken, bright.

Silent dreams begin to stir,
Whispers soft as air.
In the quiet of the moment,
We find solace there.

Beyond the chaos surrounding,
A calmness takes its flight.
In the stillness of our hearts,
We embrace the whispers of night.

Stardust in the Alleyways

In shadows where whispers rest,
Dreams flicker like fireflies bright.
The moon weaves tales through the dark,
Stardust dances, igniting the night.

Forgotten corners shelter hope,
Where echoes of laughter softly play.
Graffiti splashes colors bold,
In silent alleys, dreams find their way.

Each step a heartbeat, a secret kept,
Worn bricks hold stories untold.
Forgotten paths where passion sleeps,
Awakening softly as stars unfold.

In the stillness, magic brews,
Whispers blend with the evening air.
Stardust settles on weary souls,
In alleyways, wonder lingers there.

The Echoing Silence of Ambition

In halls of glass, dreams collide,
Whispers of wishes drift along.
Hearts race like trains on the track,
The silence hides a steady song.

Motivation glimmers bright,
While shadows stretch on the floor.
Each goal a mountain to conquer,
In the silence, they yearn for more.

Glimmers of futures, of greatness sought,
Carved in the stone of resolve.
Though echoes fade, the fire remains,
In ambition's grip, we ever evolve.

The silence echoes, a deafening roar,
In the midst of chaos, we strive.
With hope as our compass, we navigate,
Through the twilight of dreams kept alive.

Visions Camouflaged in Brick

In the urban jungle, colors blend,
Dreams muffled by walls so grey.
Visions thrive in unnoticed cracks,
Where sunlight dances, shadows play.

Brick by brick, stories are laid,
Hearts buried in concrete might.
Yet in the fabric of the city,
Hope weaves through, a guiding light.

The graffiti blooms in vibrant hues,
Messages whispered through the storm.
Camouflaged hopes, hidden and plain,
Waiting for the world to transform.

Among the ruins, wonders breath,
In the silence, secrets unfurl.
Visions linger in the air, alive,
Camouflaged dreams in a bustling whirl.

Journey Through Flickering Lights

Under the glow of streetlamps bright,
We wander beneath the velvet sky.
With each flicker, a moment passes,
In the city's pulse, we learn to fly.

Footsteps echo on cobbled stones,
As laughter carries through the night.
Each shadow tells a tale unspoken,
In the dance of the dark, we find our light.

With every flicker, a heartbeat shared,
A connection, fleeting yet deep.
Journeying through the urban maze,
Awakening dreams from the sleep.

Stars above begin to shimmer,
While hearts ignite in hopeful sight.
Through the flickering, we discover,
Our paths are paved in starlit flight.

Where Ambitions Bloom

In gardens where dreams take flight,
Seeds of hope find the light.
With every challenge, they rise,
Reaching up to the skies.

Tending to passions like flowers,
Growing stronger through the hours.
Roots deep in fertile ground,
In such soil, dreams abound.

Whispers of courage we hear,
Nurtured with love, free of fear.
Each petal tells a tale,
Of ambition that will prevail.

In the sun's warm embrace,
They find their rightful place.
Where visions come to be seen,
In the heart where ambitions glean.

Hopes in High-Rise Reflections

Skyscrapers stretch toward the blue,
Mirroring dreams that feel new.
In glass and metal they gleam,
Housing our brightest dreams.

Elevators soar, taking flight,
Carrying hopes into the night.
Each floor tells a story bright,
Of aspirations in full sight.

Windows reflect our confidence,
In each glimmer, a consequence.
Hopes rise higher as we strive,
In this urban hive, we thrive.

From rooftops, the city glows,
Illuminated by the hopes we chose.
In each heartbeat, a connection,
Underneath the high-rise reflection.

Under the Urban Canopy

Beneath the trees of concrete hue,
Life pulses with dreams anew.
Sidewalks host tales untold,
In the arms of the brave and bold.

Subway lines weave through the night,
Carrying souls, chasing light.
Every journey a quest divine,
In the shadows, we intertwine.

Streetlamps flicker with desire,
Fueling our hearts, igniting fire.
Under the urban green embrace,
We find a moment of grace.

Together we dance, we explore,
Through bustling streets, we soar.
In the canopy, we understand,
Life unfolds in this vibrant land.

Luminous Paths of Possibility

In the twilight, paths ignite,
Guiding us with reflected light.
Each step is a chance to be,
In the glow of possibility.

Sidewalks shimmer with the stars,
Where dreams can mend their scars.
With hope as our guiding flame,
We find strength in the name of change.

Footprints mark the journey ahead,
Every choice, a thread we've spread.
A tapestry of fate and chance,
Inviting us to take a dance.

Through the darkness, we will roam,
Finding our way back home.
For in each spark, we choose to see,
Luminous paths of possibility.

A Canvas of Dreams in the Sky

Waves of color brush the day,
Clouds drift softly, drifting away.
Stars peek out, a guiding light,
In the sky, our dreams take flight.

Soft whispers of hope intertwine,
In the twilight, hearts align.
Each hue tells tales of our desires,
Lighting the night with quiet fires.

With every sunset, a new begin,
Pastel skies where dreams have been.
The canvas stretches, vast and wide,
Inviting souls to take a ride.

As the moon reigns, shadows sway,
In this realm, we find our way.
A canvas painted bright and bold,
Infinite stories yet untold.

Metropolis of Whispers

Beneath the towers, secrets flow,
In every corner, stories grow.
Silent echoes fill the night,
Whispers hover, taking flight.

Concrete giants touch the sky,
In their shadows, dreams comply.
Voices murmur through the haze,
A city wrapped in mystic ways.

Streets alive with muted sounds,
Life pulsates in these grounds.
Hidden truths in alleyways,
Speak of futures and bygone days.

Glimmers flicker, lost in time,
Each heartbeat a distant chime.
Metropolis, vast and deep,
In your arms, the world we keep.

Skylines Bathed in Hope

Dawn breaks soft with tender light,
Gold and amber chase the night.
Skylines rise with whispers pure,
A promise held in every cure.

Each window glows like a star,
Reflecting dreams from near and far.
The city breathes with each new day,
A canvas where our hopes will play.

Birds take flight to greet the sun,
In this dance, all fears are shunned.
With every step upon the street,
We find the rhythm, feel the beat.

Together we will forge the path,
Celebrate love, escape the wrath.
Skylines bathed in golden hue,
In every heart, a vision true.

Echoes of the Urban Heart

In the pulse of the bustling streets,
Life intertwines and softly meets.
Voices blend in a symphony,
Echoes form a vibrant spree.

Neon lights like stars at night,
Painting shadows with their light.
Every corner, a tale to share,
In this city, dreams laid bare.

Raindrops tap on window panes,
Rhythms weave through joyful strains.
The urban heart, alive and true,
Every heartbeat speaks to you.

In the silence, find your place,
Among the noise, a gentle grace.
Echoes linger in the air,
In this dance, we lay ourselves bare.

The Language of Skyscrapers

Steel and glass, they touch the sky,
Whispering dreams as days go by.
Silent stories etched in stone,
Echoes of lives, they call their own.

Windows gleam with morning light,
Casting shadows, bold and bright.
Each structure stands, a tale to share,
Of hopes and fears, floating in air.

In the night, they flicker and glow,
City lights like stars in a row.
Together they dance, a concrete ballet,
As time weaves on, night turns to day.

Language of heights, where people soar,
In every heart, they open a door.
Skyscrapers speak, if we choose to hear,
A symphony of progress, loud and clear.

Countless Visions on the Horizon

Dawn breaks softly, a canvas wide,
Promises whispered with each tide.
Colors burst as dreams take flight,
Endless visions greet the light.

Mountains loom in the distance afar,
Guiding souls like a silent star.
Paths unwind, inviting the brave,
To chase the futures they wish to save.

Waves crash down on sandy shores,
Echoes of hope in ancient roars.
Each footstep tells of journeys begun,
Countless visions 'neath the sun.

As dusk descends, the sky ablaze,
Hearts ignite in a wondrous maze.
Chasing dreams with open eyes,
We find ourselves in the endless skies.

Shadows As Stars in Disguise

In the twilight, shadows play,
Dancing softly, fading gray.
Stars emerge in the night's embrace,
Veiling dreams with hidden grace.

Whispers linger in the dark,
Silent echoes leave their mark.
Each fleeting shadow, a fleeting sigh,
Stars that twinkle, shy and spry.

Underneath the moon's soft glow,
Mysteries stir, and spirits flow.
Shadows wear their starry masks,
Life's true essence, a task unasked.

In quiet moments, truth will hide,
Beneath the stars, they softly bide.
As shadows blend with night's allure,
Stars stand witness, pure and sure.

The Pulse Beneath the Pavement

Beneath the streets, a heartbeat lies,
Hidden life where silence flies.
The city hums, a vibrant tune,
Echoing dreams like a whispered rune.

Trains rumble deep, a distant roar,
Life unfolds through each closed door.
Stories gather in the seams,
A pulse that breathes within our dreams.

Cracks in concrete reveal the past,
Moments fleeting, shadows cast.
With every step, we feel the beat,
Of lives entwined where journeys meet.

Listen close, the city's song,
In every heart, we all belong.
The pulse beneath, a call to roam,
In every stride, we find our home.

Hopes Carved into Concrete

In the city where shadows dwell,
Dreams like graffiti tell,
Hope carved deep, a silent shout,
Concrete jungles, never doubt.

With every crack, a story grows,
Each step taken, the heart knows,
Chasing light in the darkest streets,
Resilience blooms where concrete meets.

Faded marks of those who've tried,
In their efforts, hope won't hide,
Underneath the city's gaze,
Tomorrow's light, a hopeful blaze.

From the ground, we rise anew,
Each step forward, a breakthrough,
In the silence, we will sing,
Hopes carved in stone, forever spring.

Nightfall Over Neon Dreams

Underneath the neon glow,
City pulses, dreams in tow,
Whispers dance on city air,
Nightfall brings a spark to dare.

Stars are dimmed by urban lights,
As the past meets future sights,
Rolling tides of vibrant hues,
In the chaos, dreams infuse.

Moments fleeting, seconds blend,
Night unravels, we transcend,
With each heartbeat, visions stream,
In the darkness, chase the dream.

Holding tight to fleeting hopes,
On this journey, learn to cope,
As the city breathes and sighs,
Nightfall falls, we reach for skies.

Whispers of Tomorrow's Skyline

In the silence of dawn's first light,
Promises weave in the sky so bright,
Whispers carried by gentle breeze,
Tomorrow's skyline, a heart appease.

Buildings rise where dreams collide,
In their shadows, hopes confide,
Each window glimmers with visions clear,
A future bright, no room for fear.

Echoes of laughter paint the air,
In vibrant hues, no room for despair,
As we reach for the heights unknown,
Whispers guide us, we've grown.

In the tapestry of urban seams,
We find solace in shared dreams,
Tomorrow waits with open arms,
As whispers of tomorrow bring charms.

The Rising Tide of Potential

With the sun brings a fresh new day,
Waves of promise, come what may,
Each heartbeat, a sound so grand,
The rising tide, we make our stand.

As the ocean meets the shore,
Endless possibilities to explore,
In each crest, a chance to grow,
Potential swells in ebb and flow.

Ride the waves of change and chance,
In every stumble, find the dance,
Lift your eyes to the vast expanse,
The tide rises, join the trance.

Together we flow, hand in hand,
In this journey, we take a stand,
The rising tide, forever near,
Potential blossoms without fear.

Heartbeats of the Asphalt

Underneath the city glow,
Silent stories ebb and flow.
Footsteps dance on concrete dreams,
Life unfolds in vibrant streams.

Worn out soles on paths we tread,
Whispers of the life we've led.
Each heartbeat echoes in the maze,
Resilient souls in urban haze.

Lifelines drawn in asphalt gray,
Chasing shadows of the day.
Every crack holds tales untold,
Secrets buried, brave and bold.

Night falls soft with stars above,
In the dark, we find our love.
As the city breathes and sighs,
Heartbeats rise beneath the skies.

Streets of Ambition

Fields of dreams stretch far and wide,
Chasing visions, hearts collide.
Streets alive with hopes aglow,
Every corner, seeds we sow.

Bridges built with courage strong,
Voices raised in vibrant song.
With each step, our spirits soar,
No retreat, we seek for more.

Through the storm and through the strife,
We pursue the pulse of life.
With passion driving every stride,
In these streets, our dreams abide.

City lights, a bright parade,
Guiding paths that we have made.
In this race, we must ignite,
The flame of dreams, our shining light.

Echoes in the Alley

Between the bricks, shadows play,
Memories in twilight sway.
Whispers linger, stories weave,
In the silence, we believe.

Graffiti blooms with colors bright,
Art of voices lost to night.
Each echo tells of joy and pain,
Laughter mingles with the rain.

Lives collide beneath the stars,
Streetlamps glow like distant cars.
In this alley, time stands still,
Heartbeats match the city's thrill.

Footsteps soft on cobblestone,
Every shadow finds a home.
In the heart, true stories dwell,
Echoes rise, a timeless bell.

Neon Horizons

Under neon skies we roam,
Each bright light a path to home.
Dreamers chase the pulse of night,
In the glow, we find our flight.

Endless highways, bright and bold,
Tales of wanderers retold.
Every sign, a guide to seek,
In their glow, our spirits speak.

Stars reflect in windows wide,
City life, our hearts collide.
With each breath, we break the mold,
Chasing visions yet untold.

As horizons stretch like dreams,
Life is more than what it seems.
In the neon, hope ignites,
We are flames in endless nights.

Dreams in the Skyscraper

In the heights where wishes soar,
Whispers echo, dreams implore.
Caught in gold and silver beams,
Life unfolds in vibrant dreams.

Windows gleam with tales untold,
Every moment, hearts unfold.
Shadows dance in fleeting light,
Chasing sparks that burn so bright.

Elevators rise with hope,
Reaching high, we learn to cope.
Up above, the world looks small,
In this realm, we dare to fall.

Mountains made from glass and steel,
In the skyline, fates conceal.
Through the clouds, ambitions race,
In the heights, we find our place.

Paved Pathways of Desire

On the streets where dreams collide,
Every step, a passion's guide.
Brick by brick, we carve our fate,
Walk with me, there's no debate.

Chasing shadows, hearts entwine,
Paved with hope, a path divine.
Every heartbeat, every sigh,
Together, we could touch the sky.

Cobblestones like whispers call,
In the night, we stand so tall.
Each direction, choices spin,
Finding joy in where we've been.

Underneath the moonlit glow,
Feel the warmth in every flow.
Hand in hand, we'll brave the night,
On this road, our dreams take flight.

Lost in Urban Labyrinths

In the maze of concrete dreams,
Twisted paths and silent screams.
Every alley tells a tale,
Whispered hopes begin to pale.

Through the fog, I wander lost,
Counting up the endless cost.
Graffiti sings of lives once lived,
In the chaos, truth is sieved.

Streetlights flicker, guiding light,
In this darkness, search for sight.
Past the corners, shadows weave,
In the urban night, believe.

Every turn, a chance to find,
Fragments of a hopeful mind.
In this labyrinth, we'll unite,
Together, we'll ignite the night.

The Pulse of Steel and Glass

Hear the hum of city life,
A symphony, both calm and rife.
Steel and glass, they pulse and sway,
In their rhythm, hopes convey.

Bridges arch like dreams above,
Connecting hearts that seek for love.
In the clatter, voices rise,
Echoes sing beneath the skies.

Moments captured, time in flight,
Dancing shadows, day to night.
With each heartbeat, life expands,
In this city, fate commands.

Amidst the roar, we find our peace,
In the chaos, voices cease.
The pulse of steel and dreams alive,
In this urban heart, we strive.

Dreamscapes Beneath Neon Lights

In the city's pulse, vivid dreams grow,
Colors dance softly, shadows flow.
Whispers of hope in the midnight air,
Secrets unravel, everywhere.

Neon glow sparkles on rain-soaked streets,
Footsteps echo where silence meets.
Hearts entwined under a glowing sign,
Living stories, where souls align.

Floating through night on zephyr wings,
Through crowded corners, freedom sings.
Stars reflected in puddles deep,
In this realm, our dreams we keep.

A haven of wonder, where we unite,
Lost in the magic of the night.
Guided by lanterns, we wander far,
In this dreamscape, you are my star.

Concrete Visions of Tomorrow

Steel and stone rise to touch the sky,
Hope in the heart, ambitions high.
Pavements carved with tales untold,
Future whispers in the city's hold.

Dreams cast in shadows, echo clear,
Voices of the past linger near.
Wires entwined like souls intertwined,
A glimpse of tomorrow, bright and blind.

Children play where the giants stand,
Building castles from grains of sand.
Concrete rivers flowing through the town,
Visions of progress never drown.

In twilight's glow, new paths appear,
Each footstep leads to something dear.
A cycle of dreams we dare to chase,
In concrete visions, we find our place.

Metaphors in Stone and Steel

Chiseled hearts in a sculptor's hand,
Beauty born from a silent stand.
Iron veins in structures bold,
Breath of life in forms of gold.

Bridges arch like a lover's embrace,
Connecting souls in a timeless space.
Walls whisper tales of love and loss,
In every crack, we find the gloss.

Rusty memories in every beam,
Fractured echoes of a dream.
Yet within the grip of cold, hard steel,
Warmth resides, endlessly real.

Through the lens of stone, we see,
Metaphors of what we can be.
In every corner, a story waits,
Unfolding slowly, our fates.

Urban Odyssey of the Soul

Through bustling streets where shadows play,
We lose ourselves, then find the way.
Voices rise in a symphony loud,
A unity woven in a vibrant crowd.

Paths intersect, lives intertwine,
Moments of magic in every line.
Each glance carries a tale profound,
In this city's heart, connections abound.

With every step, the stories weave,
An urban tapestry we believe.
Finding solace in stranger's eyes,
In the chaos, the spirit flies.

Guided by dreams, we take the chance,
In every heartbeat, there's a dance.
An odyssey through the city's soul,
Together we journey, together we're whole.

The Alchemy of Night and Day

In the cradle of dawn, whispers arise,
Painting the sky with golden surprise.
Shadows retreat as the sun makes its claim,
Night's gentle secrets fade, never the same.

As dusk approaches, stars start to gleam,
The world quiets down, wrapped in a dream.
Moonlight dances on silvered leaves,
In this alchemy, the heart never grieves.

Whispers Among the Towers

In the city of glass, echoes collide,
Where whispers of stories and shadows abide.
Towers stand tall, like sentinels of time,
Holding the secrets, a rhythm, a rhyme.

Beneath the bright lights, lives intertwine,
Each window a glimpse, a narrative line.
Voices cascade like rain on the ground,
Together they rise, in harmony found.

Mirages Amidst the Skyscrapers

In the heat of the day, illusions take flight,
Skyscrapers shimmer in blinding sunlight.
Mirages swirl, beckoning the brave,
A dance of reflections, the heart tries to save.

As twilight descends, the colors ignite,
Figures emerge in the softening light.
What's real? What's not? In this urban expanse,
A tapestry woven, illusions in trance.

The Search for Lost Skylines

Amidst the tall buildings, memories fade,
Lost in the hustle, the dreams we once laid.
In alleys of echoes, I wander and pine,
Seeking the silhouettes of a past divine.

The sunset paints stories, once vibrant, now dim,
I chase the lost skylines, on love's fragile whim.
In the heart of the city, ghosts start to play,
Whispering softly, of night blending day.

Chasing Futures Through City Streets

Life rushes past in neon glow,
Dreams tick like clocks in swift tempo.
Beneath the hustle, hopes unfold,
Each step a story yet untold.

Shadows dance on pavement grey,
Voices echo, then drift away.
In every corner, futures gleam,
Chasing whispers of forgotten dreams.

Through alleys dark, ambition weaves,
Paths entwined, the heart believes.
With every heartbeat, visions flare,
Chasing futures, lost in prayer.

As dawn breaks on the busy scene,
The city hums, alive, serene.
In every corner, we pursue,
A world of promise, bright and new.

Urban Labyrinths of Longing

Concrete jungles, veiled in mist,
Lost in crowds, a fleeting tryst.
Every corner hides a sigh,
Echoes of dreams that slip by.

Wanderers tread on winding paths,
Chasing solace, dodging wrath.
In silent streets where shadows creep,
The city holds its secrets deep.

Flickering lights, the heart takes flight,
Every face a story, day or night.
Longing hangs thick in the air,
In urban dreams, we meet despair.

Yet amidst the chaos, hope remains,
Through twists and turns, love sustains.
In this maze, we seek to find,
Connections forged, heart intertwined.

Canvas of a Thousand Stories

Brushstrokes dance on streets so wide,
Each step a tale, with hearts as guide.
The colors blend with every stride,
A canvas where our dreams collide.

Whispers float in vibrant hues,
Lost in the tales that life imbues.
Every face a mystery spun,
A tapestry of dreams begun.

Graffiti shouts of lives unheard,
In splashes bold, the heart is stirred.
A gallery of wanderers' art,
In every line, a beating heart.

Underneath the painted skies,
There lies the truth behind the lies.
In this canvas, life's a play,
Where stories merge, both night and day.

Beneath the Steel Canopy

Underneath the steel canopy,
The city breathes, pulses loud.
Echoes of footsteps hurry by,
While dreams soar beneath the shroud.

Concrete towers scrape the sky,
Whispers travel on the breeze.
Lost moments flit and fly,
Like leaves stirred in the trees.

Sunlight flickers through the grey,
Painting shadows on the ground.
In this maze, we find our way,
Stepping softly, heart profound.

Beneath the canopy of steel,
We roam where whispers weave.
In the thrumming urban feel,
Hope glimmers, we believe.

Shadows of a Thousand Dreams

In the quiet of the night,
Shadows dance on cobblestones.
Every whisper holds a dream,
Every sigh, a heart alone.

Underneath the silver moon,
Flickers of ambition glow.
Echoes of a hidden tune,
Guiding souls where wishes flow.

Through the alleys, secrets hide,
Voices blend with night's embrace.
In these lanes, where hopes collide,
Shadows carve a timeless space.

A tapestry of longing spun,
With threads of stories shared.
A tapestry that's never done,
In dreams, we find we're bared.

Voices of the Asphalt Jungle

In the asphalt jungle's heart,
Voices rise, a vibrant hum.
Stories woven, lives apart,
In the chaos, we become.

Horns are blaring, footsteps quick,
Every face tells tales of strife.
In the pulse, we find the trick,
Life unfolds, a vibrant life.

Neon lights paint hope anew,
Casting shadows in the dark.
In this maze, we find what's true,
In the rush, we leave our mark.

Voices whisper, voices shout,
Every corner holds a dream.
In this grind, we learn about,
Life's mosaic, a shared theme.

Gates to Infinite Horizons

At the gates to infinite skies,
Wonders wait for those who seek.
Boundless dreams in quiet sighs,
Every journey, a path unique.

With each step, the world unfolds,
Horizons stretch, inviting light.
Stories linger, softly told,
In the dawn, cast shadows bright.

Through the gates, we chase the stars,
Where the infinite calls our name.
Beneath the moons and glowing mars,
All our spirits fan the flame.

Every heart beats with the quest,
To explore what lies beyond.
In the vastness, we find rest,
As horizons whisper fond.

Secrets Revealed After Dusk

Whispers linger in the dark,
Shadows dance beneath the trees.
A chill runs down the spine,
As truths float on the breeze.

Moonlight spills on hidden paths,
Casting light on secrets old.
Each star a watcher in the night,
Stories waiting to be told.

Curtains fall, the world is hushed,
Eyes are drawn to distant sounds.
In the quiet, hearts unlock,
Old scars fade, new love surrounds.

With dawn's breath, the tales retreat,
But lingering dreams still glow.
The night reveals what day conceals,
In dusk's embrace, we truly know.

Urban Mythologies in Dreams

Concrete jungles twist and turn,
Legends echo in the night.
Footsteps chase the tales we learn,
As shadows paint a fleeting sight.

Subway whispers, critical paths,
Lost souls wander seeking truth.
Ghostly grips in crowded laughs,
Memories cling, eternal youth.

Every corner holds a story,
Each alley wraps in a sigh.
Modern myths hold hidden glory,
In dreams we question, dare to fly.

City lights surrender softly,
To voices hidden in the seams.
In urban night, we wander often,
Exploring life through tangled dreams.

Glistening Hopes on Every Corner

Amid the hustle, sparks ignite,
A hopeful glow from every stand.
Dreamers gather, hearts alight,
Each moment brimming, unplanned.

Buskers strum beneath the stars,
Their melodies float, sweet and free.
Coins drop in, a symphony,
Love threads weave through harmony.

In crowded streets where stories blend,
Each eye reflects a different fate.
A woven tapestry we mend,
As hand in hand, we celebrate.

Glistening hopes dance in the night,
Around each corner, passions spark.
In the heartbeat of the city's light,
Together we'll leave our mark.

Threads of Destiny in the City

Golden threads through concrete span,
Binding souls in silent grace.
Each encounter, part of the plan,
In this vast, unending space.

Streetlamps flicker, stories unfold,
Fates intertwine at every step.
Journeys marked in silver and gold,
Dreams forgotten, secrets kept.

A tapestry of lives we weave,
With every choice, a pathway drawn.
Through the chaos, we believe,
In the dawn, our fears are gone.

The city breathes, a vibrant song,
Threads of destiny intertwine.
In its arms, we all belong,
Our stories inked by design.

Chronicles of an Electric Dawn

A spark ignites the waking sky,
With hues of gold that seem to fly.
The world, awash in vibrant light,
Receives the day, dispelling night.

Whispers of dreams float on the breeze,
Inviting hearts to feel at ease.
Each heartbeat syncs with morning's song,
A symphony where we belong.

Through ancient streets, on pathways bright,
Hope dances boldly in the light.
Electric tales weave through the air,
Guiding souls with love and care.

As shadows fade and spirits gleam,
Awakening to each new dream.
The dawn, a canvas rich and deep,
Embracing truths we vow to keep.

The Canvas of Crowded Streets

In bustling corners, colors blend,
With stories shared around each bend.
Voices rise, a vibrant song,
Where busy hearts and dreams belong.

Sidewalks breath with tales untold,
Of strangers meeting, hands to hold.
A dance of life, both fast and slow,
In every glance, new seeds to sow.

From morning rush to evening glow,
The city hums, a constant flow.
Each passerby, a fleeting star,
Merging dreams, no matter how far.

Brush-strokes paint the lives we weave,
In crowded streets, we dare believe.
That through the chaos, love will rise,
A masterpiece 'neath urban skies.

Silhouettes of Aspiration

In fleeting shadows cast by light,
Our dreams take shape, prepare for flight.
Each silhouette whispers of grace,
Chasing visions we yearn to embrace.

With every leap strikes a chord,
As hopes are chased, and fears ignored.
The path ahead may twist and turn,
Yet through our veins, ambition burns.

In quiet moments, doubts may swell,
Yet echoes of strength compel.
For in the night, our spirits soar,
Shaping futures, we will explore.

Together we rise in unison's cry,
Finding courage as stars draw nigh.
Silhouettes dancing, bold and free,
Awakening what we're meant to be.

Lanterns in the Twilight

When day surrenders, shadows blend,
Soft lanterns sparkle, night extends.
They flicker softly, guiding the way,
Through whispered hopes at end of day.

Voices linger in twilight's hush,
As stars awaken, bright and lush.
Beneath their gaze, our dreams take flight,
Embracing warmth of the gentle night.

Each glow a promise, a tale unsung,
Of hearts united, forever young.
With every flicker, fears release,
In lantern light, we find our peace.

Together we walk, hand in hand,
Through shimm'ring worlds, with dreams so grand.
Lanterns shining, we will ignite,
A tapestry woven, bold and bright.

Milton Keynes UK
Ingram Content Group UK Ltd.
UKHW020740071024
449371UK00014B/957

9 789916 881354